# Alfred's Kid's Ukulele Cour[se] Complete

## The Easiest Ukulele Method Ever!

### Ron Manus • L. C. Harnsberger

**Alfred Music**
P.O. Box 10003
Van Nuys, CA 91410-0003
alfred.com

ISBN-10: 0-7390-9366-5 (Book & Online Audio)
ISBN-13: 978-0-7390-9366-5 (Book & Online Audio)

ISBN-10: 0-7390-9367-3 (Book & DVD & Online Video/Audio)
ISBN-13: 978-0-7390-9367-2 (Book & DVD & Online Video/Audio)

*Cover and interior illustrations by Jeff Shelly.*
*Ukulele photo courtesy of Martin Guitars.*
*Photos on page 8 by Jennifer Harnsberger Photography, jhphotostudio.com.*

**ONLINE ACCESS INCLUDED**

*Stream or download the audio content for this book. To access online audio, visit:* **www.alfred.com/redeem**

*Enter the following code:* 00-40521_882288

**Special thanks to our families, friends, and especially Jennifer, Genevieve, Patrese, and Catherine Harnsberger.**

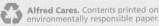

**Alfred Cares.** Contents printed on environmentally responsible paper.

# Contents

The companion online audio contains all the warm-ups and tunes in *Alfred's Kid's Ukulele Complete*, for you to listen to and play along with. See page 1 for information on how to access the audio files.

# Selecting Your Ukulele

Ukuleles come in different types and sizes. There are four basic sizes: soprano, concert, tenor, and baritone. The smallest is the soprano, and they get gradually bigger, with the baritone being the largest.

| Soprano | Concert | Tenor | Baritone |

Soprano, concert, and tenor ukes are all tuned to the same notes, but the baritone is tuned to different notes. Each uke has a different sound. The soprano has a light, soft sound, which is what you expect when you hear a ukulele. The larger the instrument, the deeper the sound is. Some tenor ukuleles have six or even eight strings.

The soprano ukulele is the most common, but you can use soprano, concert, and four-string tenor ukuleles with this book. Because the baritone uke is tuned to the same notes as the top four strings of the guitar, you can use *Alfred's Kid's Guitar Method Book 1* to start learning on that type of ukulele.

# Parts of the Ukulele

Headstock

Tuning pegs

Nut

Strings

Fretboard
(includes all
frets)

Fret wire

Soundhole

Waist

Bridge

## Caring for Your Ukulele

Get to know your ukulele and treat it like a friend. When you carry it, think of it as part of your body so you don't accidentally bump it against walls or furniture, and be especially sure not to drop it! Every time you are done playing, carefully dust off your ukulele with a soft cloth, and be sure to put it away in its case. If you don't have a case, always put it in a safe place where it won't be in the way.

# Tuning Your Ukulele

First make sure your strings are wound properly around the tuning pegs. They should go from the inside to the outside, as in the picture.

Turning a tuning peg clockwise makes the pitch lower. Turning a tuning peg counter-clockwise makes the pitch higher. Be sure not to tune the strings too high because they could break!

higher          higher

3rd String C          2nd String E

lower          lower

4th String G          1st String A

## Important:

Always remember that the string closest to the floor is the 1st string. The one closest to the ceiling is the 4th string.

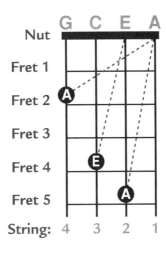

Ceiling

4th String

Floor

1st String

## Tuning with the Audio Tracks

Books 1 & 2  Tracks 1 & 2

### Using Audio Tracks
Access the online audio (see inside front cover), and play Tracks 1 and 2. Listen to the directions and match each of your ukulele's strings to its pitch on the audio tracks.

### Using Your DVD
Put the DVD in your computer or DVD player. Go to the Scenes menu and click on Tuning. Follow the directions and listen carefully to get your ukulele in tune.

## Tuning without the Audio Tracks or DVD

### Tuning the Ukulele to Itself
When your 1st string is in tune, you can tune the rest of the strings just using the ukulele alone. First tune the 1st string to A on the piano, then follow the instructions to the right to get the ukulele in tune.

Press fret 5 of string 2 and tune it to the pitch of string 1 (A).

Press fret 4 of string 3 and tune it to the pitch of string 2 (E).

Press fret 2 of string 4 and tune it to the pitch of string 1 (A).

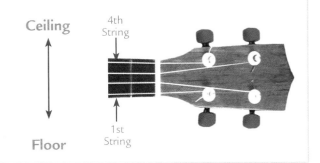

|  | G | C | E | A |
|---|---|---|---|---|
| Nut |  |  |  |  |
| Fret 1 |  |  |  |  |
| Fret 2 | A |  |  |  |
| Fret 3 |  |  |  |  |
| Fret 4 |  |  | E |  |
| Fret 5 |  |  |  | A |
| String: | 4 | 3 | 2 | 1 |

### Pitch Pipes and Electronic Tuners
If you don't have a piano available, buying an electronic tuner or pitch pipe is recommended. The salesperson at your music store can show you how to use them.

# How to Hold Your Ukulele

Hold your ukulele in the position that is most comfortable for you. Some positions are shown below.

Rest the ukulele gently on your thigh.

Cradle the ukulele with your right arm by gently holding it close to your body. Your right hand should be free to strum it.

When you practice on your own or want to play just for fun, you might feel comfortable sitting cross-legged on the floor or on your bed. Just be sure to keep good posture with your back straight.

Sitting on the floor

8

# Strumming the Strings

To *strum* means to play the strings with your right hand by brushing quickly across them. There are two common ways of strumming the strings. One is with a pick, and the second is with the fingers.

## Strumming with a Pick

Hold the pick between your thumb and index finger. Hold it firmly, but don't squeeze it too hard.

Strum from the 4th string (closest to the ceiling) to the 1st string (closest to the floor).

**Start near the top string.**

**Move mostly your wrist, not just your arm. Finish near the bottom string.**

## Strumming with Your Fingers

First decide if you feel more comfortable strumming with the side of your thumb or the nail of your index finger. The strumming motion is the same with the thumb or finger as it is when using the pick. Strum from the 4th string (closest to the ceiling) to the 1st string (closest to the floor).

**Strumming with the thumb**

**Strumming with the index finger**

## Important:

Strum by mostly moving your wrist, not just your arm. Use as little motion as possible. Start as close to the top string as you can, and never let your hand move past the edge of the ukulele.

Book 1
 Track 3

# Time to Strum!

Strum all four strings slowly and evenly.
Count your strums out loud as you play.
Repeat this exercise until you feel comfortable strumming the strings.

| strum | strum | strum | strum | strum | strum | strum | strum |
|-------|-------|-------|-------|-------|-------|-------|-------|
| / | / | / | / | / | / | / | / |
| Count: 1 | 2 | 3 | 4 | 5 | 6 | 7 | 8 |

# Strumming Notation

## Beats

Each strum you play is equal to one *beat*. Beats are even, like the ticking of a clock.

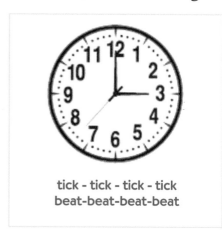

tick - tick - tick - tick
beat-beat-beat-beat

### Introducing the Quarter-Note Slash

slash

stem

1 beat

A slash with a stem is called a *quarter-note slash*. Each quarter-note slash equals one beat.

## The Staff and Treble Clef

Ukulele music is usually written on a five-line *staff* that has a *treble clef* at its beginning.

Treble clef

5
4
3
2
1

## Bar Lines, Measures, and Time Signatures

*Bar lines* divide the staff into equal parts called measures. A *double bar line* is used at the end to show you the music is finished.

Bar lines

Double bar line

measure     measure

Measures are always filled with a certain number of beats. You know how many beats are in each measure by looking at the *time signature*, which is always at the beginning of the music. A 4/4 time signature ("four-four time") means there are 4 equal beats in every measure.

Time signature

Book 1
Track 4

## More Time to Strum

Play this example in 4/4 time. It will sound the same as "Time to Strum," which you played on the previous page. Keep the beats even and count out loud.

Strum all four strings as you did before.

Strum Strum Strum Strum     Strum Strum Strum Strum

Count: 1   2   3   4     1   2   3   4

*Strumming all four strings*

# ACTIVITY: The Staff and Treble Clef

Ukulele music is usually written on a five-line *staff*.
The lines are numbered from the bottom up.

5
4
3
2
1

At the beginning of each staff
is a *treble clef* that looks like this:

## How to Draw the Treble Clef

**Step 1:**   Draw a circle under the staff and fill it in.

**Step 2:**   Draw a curved line (like the letter "u") that starts from the bottom
of the circle and touches the bottom of the first line of the staff.

**Step 3:**   Draw a line up from the first line to the fifth line.

**Step 4:**   Draw a loop above the second line of the staff.

**Step 5:**   Draw a long curving line that goes around the second line of the staff.

Now, draw six treble clefs below.

11

# ACTIVITY: Bar Lines and Measures

*Bar lines* divide the staff into equal parts called *measures.* A *double bar line* is used at the end to show you the music is finished.

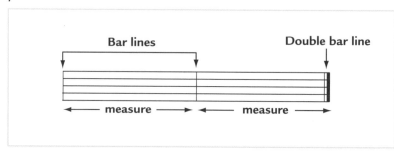

## How to Draw Measures

Draw bar lines and a double bar line.

Draw the treble clef, bar lines, and double bar line to make four measures.

Make the same four measures again.

# ACTIVITY:
# The 4/4 Time Signature

A *time signature* tells you how many beats are in a measure.
A 4/4 time signature means there are four equal beats in every measure.

## How to Draw the 4/4 Time Signature

**Step 1:** Draw a number "4" sitting on top of the third line of the staff.

**Step 2:** Draw a second "4" below the first one, sitting on the bottom line.

Now, draw six 4/4 time signatures.

# ACTIVITY:
# The Quarter-Note Slash

A slash with a stem is called a *quarter-note slash*.
Each quarter-note slash equals one beat.

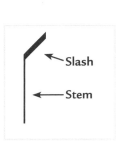

Slash

Stem

## How to Draw the Quarter-Note Slash

**Step 1:** Create the slash by drawing a slanted line from the second staff line to the fourth staff line.

**Step 2:** Create the stem by drawing a line from the bottom of the slash to just below the staff.

Now, draw six quarter-note slashes.

# ACTIVITY: Counting Time

Draw four quarter-note slashes in each measure.

Write the counts for each measure below the quarter-note slashes.

Draw four measures including a treble clef, $\frac{4}{4}$ time signature, bar lines, a double bar line, and four quarter-note slashes in each measure. Then, write the counts below the measures.

# Using Your Left Hand

## Hand Position

Learning to use your left-hand fingers easily starts with a good hand position. Place your hand so your thumb rests comfortably in the middle of the back of the neck. Position your fingers on the front of the neck as if you are gently squeezing a ball between them and your thumb. Keep your elbow in and your fingers curved.

Keep elbow in and fingers curved

Like gently squeezing a ball between your fingertips and thumb

## Placing a Finger on a String

When you press a string with a left-hand finger, make sure you press firmly with the tip of your finger and as close to the fret wire as you can without actually being right on it. Short fingernails are important! This will create a clean, bright tone.

**RIGHT**
Finger presses the string down near the fret without actually being on it.

**WRONG**
Finger is too far from fret wire; tone is "buzzy" and indefinite.

**WRONG**
Finger is on top of fret wire; tone is muffled and unclear.

## How to Read Chord Diagrams

Chord diagrams show where to place your fingers. The example to the right shows finger 1 on the 1st string at the 1st fret. The "o"s above the 2nd, 3rd and 4th strings tell you these strings are to be played open, meaning without pressing down on them with a left-hand finger.

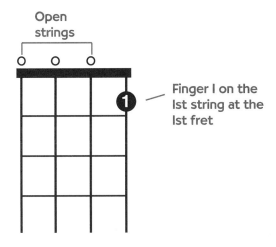

Open strings

Finger I on the Ist string at the Ist fret

# The C Chord

Use finger 3 to press the 1st string at the 3rd fret. If you have any trouble holding finger 3 down to play the C chord, place fingers 1 and 2 on the 1st and 2nd frets behind finger 3 until you are able to play with just finger 3.

## My First Chord

Book 1
Track 6

### Strumming

Strum the four-string C chord on each quarter-note slash ⌐. Make sure your strums are even. Count aloud as you play:

1–2–3–4 | 1–2–3–4.

Listen to the song on the recording to hear how it should sound!

Remember: This means there are four beats in each measure.

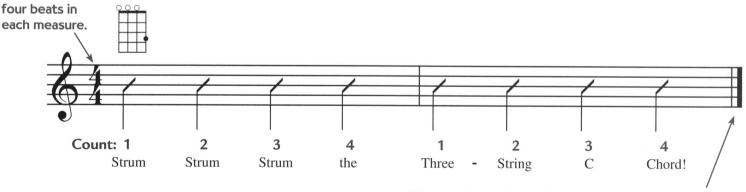

Count: 1    2    3    4    1    2    3    4

Strum   Strum   Strum   the   Three - String   C   Chord!

This **double bar line** tells us the music is finished.

# ACTIVITY: The C Chord

## Chord Diagrams

When reading a chord diagram, you will see exactly where to put your fingers. Each vertical line represents one of the four strings of the ukulele: from left to right, 4 3 2 1. An **o** above a string means it is played open (not fingered). A circled number on a string shows you which finger to use and where to place it on that string.

### C Chord

Strings:   4   3   2   1

Write the chord symbol "C" three times.

Draw the **o**'s and fingering for the C chords below.

17

# The Quarter Rest

## Introducing the Quarter Rest

1 beat

This strange-looking music symbol means to be silent for one beat. Stop the sound of the strings by lightly touching them with the side of your hand, as in the photo.

Book 1
Track 7

## Rest Warm-up

Before playing "Three Blind Mice," practice this exercise until you are comfortable playing rests.

Strum   Strum   Strum   Stop      Strum   Strum   Strum   Stop

1       2       3      (rest)      1       2       3      (rest)

## Practice Tip

Strum the chords and have a friend sing the words.

# Three Blind Mice

Book 1
Track 8   C

Count: 1        2        3       (rest)        1        2        3       (rest)        1        2        3       (rest)
      Three   blind    mice,                 Three    blind    mice,                See    how they    run.

       1        2        3       (rest)        1        2        3       (rest)        1        2        3       (rest)
      See    how they    run.                 Three    blind    mice,                Three    blind    mice.

# ACTIVITY: The Quarter Rest

**Quarter Rest**

The *quarter rest* means to be silent for one beat.

## How to Draw the Quarter Rest

**Step 1:** Draw a short line slanting down from left to right.

**Step 2:** Draw a longer line slanting down from right to left starting at the bottom of the first line.

**Step 3:** Draw another short line slanting down from left to right starting at the bottom of the second line.

**Step 4:** Draw a curled line, almost like a letter "c," starting at the bottom of the third line.

Now, draw five quarter rests.

## Counting Time

Fill in the missing beats with quarter rests.

Write the counts below the staff. Put parentheses around the counts that are for rests.

# The C⁷ Chord

**Hear this chord!**
Book 1
 Track 9

Use finger 1 to press the 1st string at the 1st fret. This chord is just like the C chord but you are using your 1st finger and not your 3rd finger.

# My Second Chord

Book 1
Track 10

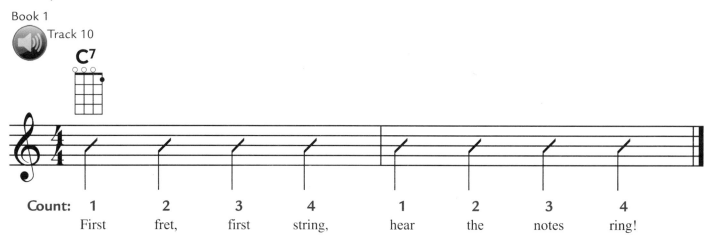

| Count: | 1 | 2 | 3 | 4 | 1 | 2 | 3 | 4 |
|---|---|---|---|---|---|---|---|---|
| | First | fret, | first | string, | hear | the | notes | ring! |

# ACTIVITY: The C⁷ Chord

## The C⁷ Chord

Finish drawing the **o**'s and fingering for the chords below.

**C⁷**

Write the chord symbol "C7" three times.

C7

_____

_____

_____

# Troubadour Song

Remember to stop the sound by lightly touching the strings with the side of your hand on each 𝄾. Wait one beat.

Book 1
Track 11

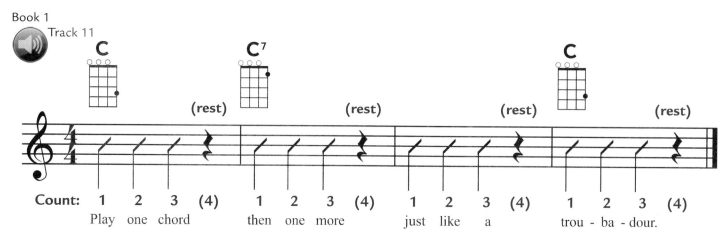

Count:  1  2  3  (4)    1  2  3  (4)    1  2  3  (4)    1  2  3  (4)

Play one chord    then one more    just like a    trou - ba - dour.

*A troubadour was a musician who traveled around singing and playing.

# The F Chord

This is the first time you are pressing two fingers down at one time. First press finger 1 on the 2nd string at the 1st fret. Then use finger 2 to press the 4th string at the 2nd fret. Press both fingers down firmly as you strum all the strings.

# My Third Chord

Book 1
Track 13

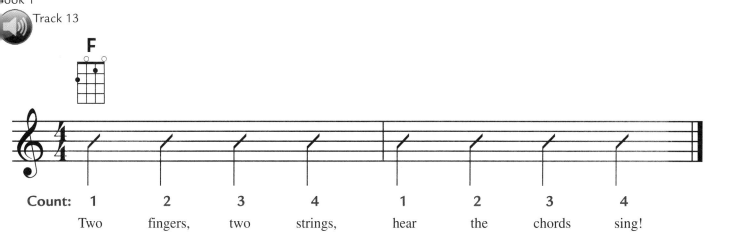

| Count: | 1 | 2 | 3 | 4 | 1 | 2 | 3 | 4 |
|---|---|---|---|---|---|---|---|---|
| | Two | fingers, | two | strings, | hear | the | chords | sing! |

# ACTIVITY:
# The F Chord

## The F Chord

Finish drawing the **o**'s and fingering for the chords below.

**F**

Write the chord symbol
"F" three times.

_____

_____

_____

# Three Chords in One Song

**F**   **C⁷**   **C**

**Remember:**

This song has three different chords in it. At first, take your time and play slowly so that all the notes sound clearly. Don't forget to be silent for a beat on each quarter rest as you change to a new chord.

## Rain Comes Down

Book 1
Track 14

**Count:** 1  2  3 (rest)   1  2  3 (rest)   1  2  3 (rest)   1  2  3  4

Tap   tap   tap,   rain comes down,   from   the sky   to   the ground. ___

(No new chord symbol, so keep playing F!)

1  2  3 (rest)   1  2  3 (rest)   1  2  3 (rest)   1  2  3 (rest)

Tap   tap   tap,   hear   the   beat.   Rain - drops   fall   all   a - round.

25

# Skip to My Lou

## Practice Tip

To change quickly from C⁷ to F in the last two measures, move your 1st finger to the 2nd string—that's not very far—and then put your 2nd finger on the 4th string.

C⁷        F        C

Book 1
Track 15

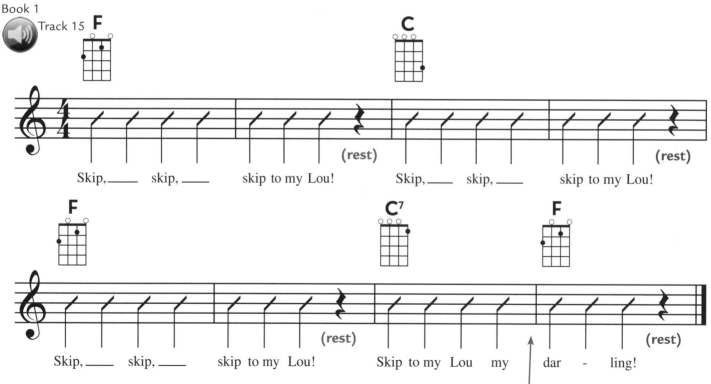

Skip,____ skip,____ skip to my Lou! (rest)    Skip,____ skip,____ skip to my Lou! (rest)

Skip,____ skip,____ skip to my Lou! (rest)    Skip to my Lou my    dar  -  ling! (rest)

Remember to move your 1st finger to the 2nd string and then put your 2nd finger on the 4th string to play the F chord on the next beat.

26

# London Bridge

Book 1

Track 16

**F**

**C**

**F**

Lon - don Bridge is    fal - ling  down,    (rest)    fal - ling  down,    (rest)    fal - ling  down    (rest)

(No new chord symbol, so keep playing F!)

**C⁷**

**F**

Lon - don Bridge   is    fal - ling  down,    (rest)    my_____ fair_____ la - dy.    (rest)

# The Repeat Sign

**Introducing Repeat Dots** :|

Double dots on the inside of a double bar line mean to go back to the beginning and play again.

## Merrily We Roll Along

Book 1

Track 17

F          C          F

Mer - ri - ly we roll a - long, roll a - long, roll a - long.

C⁷          F

Mer - ri - ly we roll a - long____ o'er the deep blue sea. _____

Repeat from the beginning

28

# ACTIVITY: The Repeat Sign

When *double dots* are written on the inside of a double bar line, it makes a *repeat sign*. A repeat sign means to go back to the beginning and play the same music again.

## How to Draw the Repeat Sign

Draw repeat signs by adding double dots to these double bar lines.

Draw a double bar line above each "Don't Repeat," and draw a repeat sign above each "Repeat."

**Repeat**     **Don't Repeat**     **Repeat**     **Repeat**     **Don't Repeat**

# Love Somebody

Book 1
Track 18

1. Love some-bod - y, yes I do! ___ Love some-bod - y, won't say who. ___
2. Love some-bod - y, want to hear? ___ Let me whis-per in your ear. ___

Love some-bod - y, can you guess? ___ Who's the one that I love best?
Love some-bod - y, now you've guessed ___ You're the one that I love best!

30

# The G⁷ Chord

**Hear this chord!**
Book 1

 Track 19

Use finger 1 to press the 2nd string at the 1st fret. Use fingers 2 and 3 to press the 3rd and 1st strings at the 2nd fret.

# My Fourth Chord

Book 1
 Track 20

For    G    sev - en,    use    three    fing - ers.

# ACTIVITY: The G⁷ Chord

**G⁷**

Write the chord symbol "G⁷" three times.

G⁷ _____ _____

Draw the **o**'s for these chords.

**G⁷**   **C⁷**   **C**   **F**

## Let's Practice Writing Music

Finish creating four measures of music by tracing the treble clefs, time signature, bar lines, quarter-note slashes, quarter rests, repeat sign, and chord frames.

# Using G⁷ with Other Chords

## Practice Tip

Before you play "A-Tisket, A-Tasket," "Aloha 'Oe," "When the Saints Go Marching In," and "Yankee Doodle," practice the exercises on this page. They will help you to change chords easily.

Play each exercise very slowly at first, and gradually play them faster. Don't move on to play the songs until you can easily move from chord to chord without missing a beat.

# A-Tisket, A-Tasket

Book 1

Track 24

A tis - ket! A tas - ket! Have you seen my

bas - ket? My moth - er sent me to the mar - ket

on the way I lost —— it! I lost —— it! My

bas - ket! Have you seen my bas - ket? For

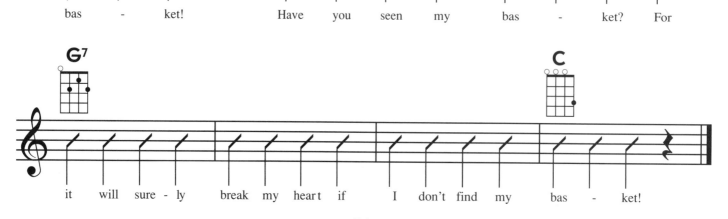

it will sure - ly break my heart if I don't find my bas - ket!

# Aloha ʻOe
# (Farewell to Thee)

Book 1
Track 25

**F**

**C**

(rest)

Fare - well to _____ thee, _____ fare - well _____ to _____

**G⁷**

thee, _____ O beau - teous one who lives a - mong the

**C**    **C⁷**    **F**

flow - ers, _____ one fond em - brace _____ be -

**C**    **G⁷**

fore _____ I _____ leave, _____ un - til _____ we

**C**

meet _____ a - gain. _____

# When the Saints Go Marching In

Book 1
Track 26

**C**

(rest) Oh when the saints————————— go march-ing in,—————

**G⁷**

—— Oh when the saints—— go—— march - ing—— in,—————

**C**   **C⁷**   **F**

—— Oh how I want———— to be—— in that num - ber—————

**C**   **G⁷**   **C**

———— When the saints—— go—— march - ing—— in.—————

36

# Yankee Doodle

Book 1
Track 27

C     G⁷     C     G⁷

Yan - kee Doo - dle went to town —— rid - ing on a po - ny, ——

C     F     G⁷     C

Stuck a fea - ther in his hat and called it mac - a - ro - ni. (rest)

F     C

Yan - kee Doo - dle keep it up, (rest) Yan - kee Doo - dle dan - dy. (rest)

F     C     G⁷     C

Mind the mu - sic and the step and with the girls be han - dy.

37

# ACTIVITY: Write Your Own Song with Four Chords

Here's your chance to write your first song. Follow these steps.

1. Draw a treble clef at the beginning of each staff.
2. Draw a $\frac{4}{4}$ time signature next to the treble clef in the first measure.
3. Fill in the bar lines and draw a repeat sign at the end.
4. Draw quarter-note slashes and quarter rests. You can choose which beats have slashes and which have rests, but be sure there are exactly four beats in each measure.
5. Choose which chords you want by filling in the chord frame above each measure.
6. Make up your own lyrics and write them below each staff.
7. **Have fun** and play your song on your ukulele.

# Getting Acquainted with Music Notation

## Notes

Musical sounds are represented by symbols called *notes*. Their time value is determined by their color (black or white), and by stems and flags attached to them.

## The Staff

Each note has a name. That name depends on where the note is found on the *staff*. The staff is made up of five horizontal lines and the spaces between those lines.

```
————————————————— 5th LINE —————————————————
                                                    4th SPACE
————————————— 4th LINE —————————————
                                            3rd SPACE
————————— 3rd LINE —————————
                                    2nd SPACE
——————— 2nd LINE ———————
                            1st SPACE
— 1st LINE ———————
```

## The Music Alphabet

The notes are named after the first seven letters of the alphabet (A–G).

A  B  C  D  E  F  G

## Clefs

As music notation progressed through history, the staff had from two to twenty lines, and symbols were invented that would always give you a reference point for all the other notes. These symbols were called *clefs*.

Music for the ukulele is written in the G or *treble clef*. Originally, the Gothic letter G was used on a four-line staff to show the pitch G.

This developed into the modern clef:

G

# ACTIVITY: The Staff

The *staff* is made up of five horizontal lines and the four spaces between those lines. The lines and spaces are numbered from the bottom up.

5th LINE
4th SPACE
4th LINE
3rd SPACE
3rd LINE
2nd SPACE
2nd LINE
1st SPACE
1st LINE

Name the line or space for each note.

__1st__ line    _____ space    _____ line    _____ space    _____ line

_____ space    _____ line    _____ space    _____ line

Name the line for each note in the box below the staff.

2nd

Name the space for each note in the box below the staff.

1st

An easy way to remember the notes on the lines is using the phrase **Every Good Bird Does Fly**. Remembering the notes in the spaces is even easier because they spell the word **FACE**, which rhymes with "space."

Notes on the lines
E    G    B    D    F

Notes in the spaces
F    A    C    E

### Introducing the Quarter Note

stem

notehead →

1 beat

A black note with a stem is called a *quarter note*. Like the quarter-note slash, the quarter note equals one beat.

Book 1
Track 28

## Clap and Count Out Loud

$\frac{4}{4}$

1   2   3   4   |   1   2   3   (4)   |   1   2   3   (4)   |   1   2   3   (4)

# ACTIVITY: The Quarter Note

A *quarter note* has a black notehead and a stem.
Each quarter note equals one beat.

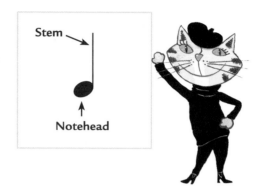

## How to Draw the Quarter Note

**Step 1:**  To create the notehead, draw an oval and fill it in.
Draw several noteheads below in the third space.

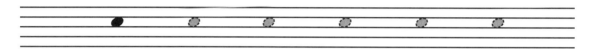

**Step 2:**  To create the stem, draw a line going down from
the left of the notehead to just below the staff.

Now, draw six quarter notes on the third space of the staff.

Now, draw six quarter notes in the second
space with the stem going up from the right of
the notehead.

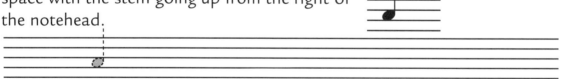

## Counting Time

Draw four quarter notes in each measure. In the first two measures, draw quarter notes
having stems down, and in the second two measures, draw quarter notes having stems up.
Then, write the counts below the staff.

# Notes on the 1st String
# Introducing A

A note sitting on the second space of the treble clef staff is called A. To play this note, pick the open 1st string (meaning without putting a left-hand finger on it).

**Hear this note!**
Book 1

Track 29

## Abby, the Armadillo

Book 1
Track 30

### Picking

- Play each A slowly and evenly, using a *downpick* motion. We will use only downpicks for the rest of the book.

- Use only a little motion to pick each note, just like strumming.

| Count: | 1 | 2 | 3 | 4 | 1 | 2 | 3 | 4 | 1 | 2 | 3 | 4 | 1 | 2 | 3 | 4 |
| --- | --- | --- | --- | --- | --- | --- | --- | --- | --- | --- | --- | --- | --- | --- | --- | --- |
| | Al | li | ga | tor | Al | ate | ap | ples | a | round | Ab | by | Ar | ma | dil | lo. |

# ACTIVITY: The Note A (1st String)

The note on the second space of the staff is called A.

## Drawing the Note A

**Step 1:** Draw an oval notehead in the second space of the staff.

**Step 2:** For the stem, draw a line from the right of the notehead to just above the top line of the staff. The stem always goes up for this note.

Now, draw the note A six times below.

## Playing the Note A

To play the note A, pick the open 1st string.

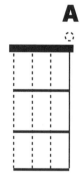

Indicate the fingering for note A by placing "**o**" above the 1st string on each diagram.

# The Note A with Chords

## Practice Tip

For this tune, remember that both the F and C$^7$ chords use finger 1 at the 1st fret.

**F Chord**          **C$^7$ Chord**

It's easy to move your finger over one string to change chords, but don't forget your 2nd finger on the 4th string.

Book 1
Track 31

### Note and Strum Warm-up
Before playing "Note and Strum" practice this exercise slowly until you are comfortable playing a note followed by a strum.

F          C$^7$

note strum strum rest    note strum strum rest

# Note and Strum

Book 1
Track 32

| Count: | 1 | 2 | 3 | (4) | 1 | 2 | 3 | (4) | 1 | 2 | 3 | (4) | 1 | 2 | 3 | (4) |
|---|---|---|---|---|---|---|---|---|---|---|---|---|---|---|---|---|

Note strum strum rest.    Note strum strum rest.    Note strum strum rest.    Note strum strum rest.

# Notes on the 1st String
# Introducing B

**Hear this note!**
Book 1
Track 33

A note on the middle line of the staff is called B. To play this note, use finger 2 to press the 1st string at the 2nd fret. Use a downpick motion to play only the 1st string.

Book 1
Track 34

## Up-Down-Up Warm-up

Before playing "Up-Down-Up," practice this exercise until you are comfortable playing the note B.

# Up-Down-Up

Book 1
Track 35

Start on A then se - cond fin - ger. Down to A then up to the B.

# ACTIVITY:
# The Note B (1st String)

The note on the middle line of the staff is called B.

## Drawing the Note B

**Step 1:**   Draw an oval notehead on the second line of the staff.

**Step 2:**   For the stem, draw a line from the left of the notehead to just below the bottom line of the staff. The stem always goes down for this note.

Now, draw the note B six times below.

**B**

## Playing the Note B

To play the note B, press the 2nd fret of the 1st string.

Indicate the fingering for note B by placing the number "2" in a circle on the 2nd fret of the 1st string on each diagram.

# The Notes A and B with Chords

## Practice Tip

For this tune, notice that the note B and the C chord are one finger apart. Finger the B with the 2nd finger on the 2nd fret of the 1st string, and then use the 3rd finger on the 3rd fret of the 1st string to play the C chord. First, just practice switching those fingers and then play the music below.

**Note B**

**C Chord**

Book 1

Track 36

A strum strum rest.    B strum strum rest.    One more time rest,    then you can rest.

# Notes on the 1st String
# Introducing C

**Hear this note!**
Book 1
Track 37

A note sitting on the third space of the treble clef staff is called C. Use finger 3 to press the 1st string at the 3rd fret. Use a downpick motion to play only the 1st string.

C

1st fret

2nd fret

3rd fret

3rd finger

Book 1
Track 38

## C Warm-up

# The Mountain Climber

Book 1
Track 39

From the bot-tom to the top, the fear-less climb-er does not stop.

With his fav-'rite uke he seeks to yo-del from the moun-tain peaks.

49

# ACTIVITY: The Note C (1st String)

The note on the third space of the staff is called C.

## Drawing the Note C

**Step 1:** Draw an oval notehead on the third space of the staff.

**Step 2:** For the stem, draw a line from the left of the notehead to just below the bottom line of the staff. The stem always goes down for this note.

Now, draw the note C six times below.

## Playing the Note C

To play the note C, press the 3rd fret of the 1st string.

Indicate the fingering for note C by placing the number "3" in a circle on the 3rd fret of the 1st string on each diagram.

# The Notes A, B, and C with Chords

## Practice Tip

Notice that the note C and the C chord are both fingered with finger 3 at the 3rd fret on the 1st string.

**Note C**

**C Chord**

Hold down the 3rd finger between the note C and the C chord.

## Brave in the Cave

Book 1

Track 40

# Notes on the 2nd String
# Introducing E

Hear this note!
Book 1
Track 41

A note on the lowest line of the staff is called E. Play the 2nd string open.

Book 1
Track 42

E Warm-up

# Two Open Strings

Book 1
Track 43

Play the E string, now, the A string. E string, A string. Keeps you think-ing

# Two-String Melody

Book 1
Track 44

Notes on two strings are fun to play. Notes on two strings, Oh! what fun!

# ACTIVITY: The Note E (2nd String)

The note on the bottom line of the staff is called E.

## Drawing the Note E

**Step 1:** Draw an oval notehead on the first line of the staff.

**Step 2:** For the stem, draw a line from the right of the notehead to just below the top line of the staff. The stem always goes up for this note.

Now, draw the note E six times below.

**E**

## Playing the Note E

To play the note E, pick the open 2nd string.

Indicate the fingering for note E by placing "**o**" above the 2nd string on each diagram.

53

# Jumping Around

Book 1

Track 45

Bounc - ing, bounc - ing,  up  and  down.   Jump - ing, jump - ing,  all  a - round.

In  the  sky, then  on  the  ground.   First  you're  lost  and  then  you're  found!

# Notes on the 2nd String
# Introducing F

**Hear this note!**
Book 1
Track 46

**F**

A note on the 1st space of the staff is called F. Use finger 1 to press the 2nd string at the 1st fret. Pick only the 2nd string.

1st finger

1st fret

2nd fret

3rd fret

Book 1
Track 47

**F Warm-up**

# Ping Pong Song

Book 1
Track 48

O - pen E string, first fin - ger F, down to E then up to F.

# Soccer Game

Book 1
Track 49

Hold

Soc - cer balls are black and white. Play all day un - til it's night.

55

# ACTIVITY: The Note F (2nd String)

The note on the first space of the staff is called F.

## Drawing the Note F

**Step 1:** Draw an oval notehead on the first space of the staff.

**Step 2:** For the stem, draw a line from the right of the notehead to the top line of the staff. The stem always goes up for this note.

Now, draw the note F six times below.

**F**

## Playing the Note F

To play the note F, press the 1st fret of the 2nd string.

Indicate the fingering for note F by placing the number "1" in a circle on the 1st fret of the 2nd string on each diagram.

# The Half Rest

## Introducing the Half Rest

This rest means do not play for two beats, which is the same as 𝄾 𝄾.

Book 1

Track 50

**Clap and Count Out Loud**

## Practice Tip

Notice that the note F and the G⁷ chord are both fingered with finger 1 at the 1st fret on the 2nd string.

In "When I Feel Best," hold the 1st finger down from the third beat of the 1st measure until the last beat of the 5th measure.

**Note F**

**G⁷ Chord**

# When I Feel Best

Book 1

Track 51

# ACTIVITY: The Half Rest

A *half rest* means do not play for two beats.

## How to Draw the Half Rest

**Step 1:**   Draw a box on top of the middle line of the staff.

**Step 2:**   Fill in the box.

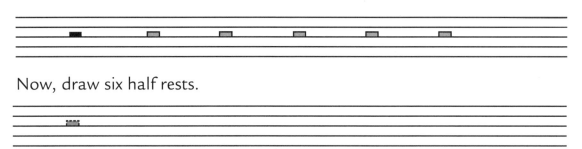

Now, draw six half rests.

## Counting Time

Fill in the missing beats with half rests.

1   2   (3)   (4)      (1)   (2)   3   4      1   2   3   4      1   2   (3)   (4)

Write the counts for each measure below the quarter-note slashes.

1   2   3   4      1

# Notes on the 2nd String
# Introducing G

Hear this note!
Book 1
 Track 52

A note on the 2nd line of the staff is called G. Use finger 3 to press the 2nd string at the 3rd fret. Pick only the 2nd string.

**G**

Ist fret

2nd fret — 3rd finger

3rd fret

③

Book 1
Track 53

## G Warm-up

## A-Choo!
Book 1
Track 54

E and F and G are eas - y. Spil - ling pep - per makes me sneez - y.

"A - a - choo! A - a - choo!" Pep - per makes me go "A - choo!"

# ACTIVITY: The Note G (2nd String)

The note on the second line of the staff is called G.

## Drawing the Note G

**Step 1:** Draw an oval notehead on the second line of the staff.

**Step 2:** For the stem, draw a line from the right of the notehead to just above the top line of the staff. The stem always goes up for this note.

Now, draw the note G six times below.

G

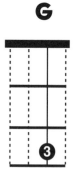

## Playing the Note G

To play the note G, press the 3rd fret of the 2nd string.

Indicate the fingering for note G by placing the number "3" in a circle on the 3rd fret of the 2nd string on each diagram.

# ACTIVITY:
# The Notes E, F, G, A, B, and C

E   F   G   A   B   C

## Reading the Notes E, F, G, A, B, and C

Write the letter name of each note in the box below the staff.

## Word Fun with Notes

Write the letter name of each note on the line below the staff. The notes in each measure spell a word!

## Drawing the Notes E, F, G, A, B, and C

Write the noteheads first, and then add the stems going down.

Now, write all six notes in order from E to C two times.

# The Half Note

## Introducing the Half Note

2 beats

This note lasts two beats.
It is twice as long as a quarter note.

Book 1

Track 55

**Clap and Count Out Loud**

# Hot Cross Buns

Book 1

Track 56

Count: 1 2 3 4 1 2 (3) (4) 1 2 3 4 1 2 (3) (4)

Hot cross buns, hot cross buns,

**Keep Counting!** One a pen - ny, two a pen - ny, hot cross buns.

# ACTIVITY: The Half Note

A *half note* lasts two beats. It is twice as long as a quarter note.

## How to Draw the Half Note

**Step 1:** Create the notehead by drawing an oval. On the staff below, draw three noteheads in the third space and three noteheads in the second space.

**Step 2:** Create the stems. For the first three notes, draw the stem going down from the left of the notehead, and for the second three notes, draw the stem going up from the right of the notehead.

Now, draw six half notes. Draw three on the third space, and three on the second space.

## Counting Time

Fill in the missing beats by adding either a half rest or a half note in each measure. Then, write the counts below the staff. Put parentheses around beats that are for rests.

# Notes on the 3rd String
# Introducing C

Hear this note! Book 1 Track 57

A line that extends the staff either up or down is called a *ledger line*. A note one ledger line below the staff is called C. You already know C on the 1st string. This C is the open 3rd string and sounds lower than C on the 1st string. To play this note, pick the open 3rd string.

**C Warm-up**

Book 1 Track 58

## Three Open Strings

Book 1
Track 59

Play C o - pen, play E o - pen, play A o - pen, E, C!

## Little Steps and Big Leaps

Book 1
Track 60

Play - ing on three strings lets me play notes far a - part.

Lit - tle steps and big leaps make my play - ing like fine art.

64

# ACTIVITY:
# The Note C (3rd String)

The note on the first ledger line below the staff is called C.

## Drawing the Note C

**Step 1:**  Draw an oval notehead on the first ledger line of the staff.

**Step 2:**  For the stem, draw a line from the right of the notehead to just above the third line of the staff. The stem always goes up for this note.

Now, draw the note C six times below.

## Playing the Note C

To play the note C, pick the open 3rd string.

Indicate the fingering for note C by placing "**o**" above the 3rd string on each diagram.

# The Old Grey Mare

Book 1

Track 61

# Notes on the 3rd String
# Introducing D

**Hear this note!**
Book 1

Track 62

A note on the space below the staff is called D. Use finger 2 to press the 3rd string at the 2nd fret. Pick only the 3rd string.

**D**

2nd finger

Book 1

Track 63

### D Warm-up

## Introducing the Whole Note

This note lasts four beats. It is as long as two half notes, or four quarter notes.

Four beats

**Clap and Count Out Loud**

Book 1

Track 64

# D Is Easy!
Book 1
Track 65

D is eas-y if you place your sec-ond fin-ger on the C string.

# Taking a Walk
Book 1
Track 66

Walk-ing up to G, then walk down to C.

**G⁷** **C**

Then I add some chords ____ so I don't get bored. ____

# ACTIVITY: The Note D (3rd String)

The note on the first space below the bottom line of the staff is called D.

## Drawing the Note D

**Step 1:** Draw an oval notehead on the space below the bottom line of the staff.

**Step 2:** For the stem, draw a line from the right of the notehead to the fourth line of the staff. The stem always goes up for this note.

Now, draw the note D six times below.

## Playing the Note D

To play the note D, pick the 2nd fret of the 3rd string.

Indicate the fingering for note D by placing the number "2" in a circle on the 2nd fret of the 3rd string on each diagram.

# ACTIVITY: The Whole Note

A *whole note* lasts four beats.

## How to Draw the Whole Note

Draw an oval in a space or on a line.

Now, draw four whole notes on spaces and four whole notes on lines.

# ACTIVITY: Review: All the Notes and Chords in Book I

Write the letter name of each note in the box below the staff.

Write the name of each chord in the box above the chord diagram.

# Ode to Joy
## from Beethoven's 9th Symphony

Book 1

 Track 67

When Bee - tho - ven wrote this tune he could not hear a sin - gle note.

But his mus - ic is so awe - some peo - ple still love things he wrote.

# Jingle Bells

Book 1
Track 68

**C**

Jin - gle bells, jin - gle bells jin - gle all the way. _____

**G⁷**

Oh what fun it is to ride a one - horse o - pen sleigh. _____

**C**

Jin - gle bells, jin - gle bells jin - gle all the way. _____

**C**

Oh what fun it is to ride a one - horse o - pen sleigh. _____

71

# Mary Had a Little Lamb

Book 1
Track 69

# Over the Rainbow

Book 1
Track 70

**Words by E. Y. Harburg**
**Music by Harold Arlen**

Some - where _____ o - ver the rain - bow

way _____ up _____ high, _____

there's _____ a _____ land that I heard of once in a

lul - la - by. _____

# Review: Music Matching Games

## Chords

Draw a line to match each chord frame on the left to the correct photo on the right.

1.

2.

3.

4.

## Symbols

Draw a line to match each symbol on the left to its name on the right.

1. o                    Treble clef

2. ♩                    Quarter note

3. ♩                    Whole note

4. ♩                    Quarter slash

5. 𝄞                    Half note

6. 𝄀                    Double bar line

7. ▬                    Half rest

8. 𝄽                    Repeat sign

9. ▬                    Quarter rest

## Notes

Draw a line to match each note on the left to its correct music notation on the right.

1.

2.

3.

4.

5.

6.

7.

8.

## Answer Key

**Chords**
1: page 23; 2: page 20; 3: page 16; 4: page 31

**Symbols**
1: page 67; 2: page 62; 3: page 41; 4: page 10;
5: page 39; 6: page 28; 7: page 57; 8: page 18;
9: page 10

**Notes**
1: page 43; 2: page 46; 3: page 49; 4: page 52
5: page 55; 6: page 59; 7: page 64; 8: page 67

74

# All the Notes I Know So Far

Book 2
Track 3

These are all the notes I know so far!

Play ing all the notes is real ly fun!

---

## Introducing the Octave

When notes have the same name but one sounds higher or lower, the notes are an octave apart. *Octave* means eight (like octopus with eight legs), so two notes with the same name but are eight notes apart are called an octave.

---

# This Is an Octave

Book 2
Track 4

This is an oct - ave. Both notes share one name.

They are just eight notes a - part. One, two, three, four, five, six, seven, eight!

# Largo

(from the *New World Symphony*)

This version of composer Antonin Dvořák's famous melody uses all the notes you know so far except one. Which note is missing?

Book 2

Track 5

Antonin Dvořák

Answer: B

76

# Dotted Half Notes & 3/4 Time

## Introducing the Dotted Half Note

Three beats

This note looks like a half note, but with a dot to the right of the notehead. It lasts three beats.

## The 3/4 Time Signature

A 3/4 time signature ("three-four time") means there are three equal beats in every measure.

The 3 on the top means there are three beats in each measure.

The 4 on the bottom means a quarter note gets one beat.

Book 2

Track 6

## Clap and Count Out Loud

Count: 1  2  3    1  2  3    1  2  3    1  2  3

# Three Is for Me!

Book 2

Track 7

One, two, three. One, two, three. Three is for me!

Play - ing in three with the great - est of ease.

77

# ACTIVITY: The Dotted Half Note

The *dotted half note* lasts three beats.

## How to Draw the Dotted Half Note

**Step 1:** Draw a half note.

**Step 2:** Add a dot to the right of the notehead.

Now, draw three dotted half notes with stems going up and three dotted half notes with stems going down.

# ACTIVITY: The ¾ Time Signature

A ¾ time signature means there are three equal beats in every measure.

## How to Draw the ¾ Time Signature

**Step 1:** Draw a number "3" sitting on top of the third line of the staff.

**Step 2:** Draw a number "4" sitting on the bottom line below the number 3.

Now, draw six ¾ time signatures.

# The Farmer in the Dell

Book 2

Track 8

**C**

The far - mer in the dell,

**C**

the far - mer in the dell.

**C**

Hi! Ho! The dai - ry -

o, the far - mer in the dell.

**C**

# Beautiful Brown Eyes

Book 2
Track 9

Beau - ti - ful, beau - ti - ful brown eyes,

smil - ing right in - to my heart. But now

where are those beau - ti - ful brown eyes? Why

must we be so far a - part?

## Introducing Common Time $\mathbf{C}$

This symbol is a time signature that means the same as $\frac{4}{4}$.

$\mathbf{C} = \frac{4}{4}$ The 4 on the top means there are four beats in each measure.
The 4 on the bottom means a quarter note gets one beat.

# Old MacDonald Had a Farm

Book 2
Track 10

G7

Old Mac - Don - ald had a farm, E - I - E - I - O! And

G7

on that farm he had a uke! E I - E - I - O!

81

# ACTIVITY: Common Time

This symbol **c** is a time signature that means the same as $\frac{4}{4}$ time. There are four beats to each measure.

## How to Draw the Common Time Signature

Draw a letter "C" from the fourth line to the second line.

Now, draw six common time signatures.

## Choose the Time Signature

Each of the following examples has either three or four beats in each measure. Place either $\frac{4}{4}$, **c**, or $\frac{3}{4}$ at the beginning of each example. Use each time signature only once.

**Time Signature**

**Time Signature**

**Time Signature**

# Introducing B-flat

A *flat* ♭ lowers a note a *half step* (the distance from one fret to another is called a half step). B♭ is played one fret lower than the note B. When a flat note appears in a measure, it is still flat until the end of that measure.

**Hear this note!**
Book 2

Track 11

**1st FRET**

## Aura Lee

Book 2
Track 12

Elvis Presley recorded this folk song as a pop ballad called "Love Me Tender."

New Note B♭

# ACTIVITY: The Note B-flat

The note on the middle line of the staff with a flat ♭ symbol before it is called B♭.

## Drawing the Note B-flat

To draw the note B♭ on the staff, place the notehead on the third line, and draw the stem down to just below the staff. Then draw a small lower case "♭" just to the left of the notehead. On the staff below, draw the note B♭ six times.

## Playing the Note B♭

To play the note B♭, press the 1st string at the 1st fret.

On the diagram to the right, indicate the fingering for the note B♭ by placing the number "1" in a circle on the 1st fret of the 1st string.

## Write Your Own Song with the Notes C, D, E, F, G, A, B-flat, and C

Compose a short melody with the notes C, D, E, F, G, A, B-flat, and C. Use quarter notes, half notes, dotted half notes, and whole notes. Remember that in $\frac{4}{4}$ time, only four beats fit in each measure.

# Three-String Boogie

Book 2

Track 13

This song uses all the notes you have learned. Don't forget to listen to the audio recording first!

# Tempo Signs

A *tempo sign* tells you how fast to play the music.
Below are the three most common tempo signs.

*Andante* ("ahn-DAHN-teh") **slow**

*Moderato* ("moh-deh-RAH-toh") **moderately**

*Allegro* ("ah-LAY-groh") **fast**

# Three-Tempo Rock

Play three times: first time **Andante**, second time **Moderato**, third time **Allegro**.

Andante — Book 2 Track 14   Moderato — Book 2 Track 15   Allegro — Book 2 Track 16

Count:  1   2   3   (rest)

## Writing Tempo Signs

Write the correct tempo sign next to the speed that matches.

**slow** _____   **moderately** _____   **fast** _____

# Rockin' Uke

Book 2

 Track 17

# Good Night Ladies

Book 2 — Track 18 — Vocals & Chords   Book 2 — Track 19 — Chords Only

For this song and most of the rest of the songs in this book, you can play either the melody or chords. Your teacher can play the part you aren't playing, or you can play along with the recording.

**Moderato**

PLAY: F … … … … … … … C⁷ … … …

Good night, la - dies, Good night, la - dies,

F … … C⁷ … … F C⁷ F … … …

Good night, la - dies, We're going to leave you now.

C⁷ … … F

Mer - ri - ly we roll a - long, Roll a - long, roll a - long.

C⁷ … … F

Mer - ri - ly we roll a - long O'er the deep blue sea.

# Blues in C

# Ties

A *tie* is a curved line that connects two of the same note. When two notes are tied, don't play the second note, but keep the first note playing until the second note is done. You are really adding the two notes together.

4 beats + 1 beat = 5 beats

2 beats + 2 beats = 4 beats

## Clap and Count Out Loud

Book 2
Track 21

Count: 1  2  3  4   1  2  3  4   1  2  3  4   1  2  3  4

# Down in the Valley

Book 2
Track 22
Vocals & Chords

Book 2
Track 23
Chords Only

Down    in    the    val    -    ley,    val - ley   so

low,_____    Hang   you   head   o   -

ver,          hear   the   wind   blow. _____

Hear   the   wind   blow,        boys,       hear   the   wind

blow, _____     Hang   your   head   o   -

ver,          hear   the   wind   blow. _____

# ACTIVITY: Ties

A *tie* is a curved line that connects two of the same note. When two notes are tied, don't play the second note, but add the two notes together instead.

## How to Draw the Tie

When the notes being tied are on or above the middle line of the staff, the curve of the tie goes up.

When the notes being tied are below the middle line of the staff, the curve of the tie goes down.

Draw ties to connect the notes below. Then write the total number of beats for each pair on the line below the staff.

5 beats

_____

_____

_____

_____

_____

# Key Signatures

The *key signature* at the beginning of a piece tells you when a note is played as a flat note throughout the piece. In "Ode to Joy," each B is played as B-flat.

## Ode to Joy (Extended Version)

Book 2

 Track 24
Vocals & Chords

Book 2

Track 25
Chords Only

Key Signature: remember to play each B one half step lower.

# ACTIVITY: Key Signatures

The key signature at the beginning of a piece of music tells you when a note is played as a flat note throughout the piece.

In "Ode to Joy" below, draw a blue box around all the B-flats that are on beat 2 of a measure, and draw a red box around all the B-flats that are on beat 3.

# Ode to Joy

**Moderato**

# Pickup Measures

Not all pieces of music begin on the first beat. Sometimes music begins with just part of a measure, which is called a *pickup*.

A pickup is like a pumpkin pie. If you were to cut the pie into four equal pieces and take one piece away, there would be three pieces left. If you are playing in 𝄴 time and the pickup measure has one quarter note, there will be three quarter notes in the last measure.

Playing in ¾ time is like cutting the pie into three equal pieces: if there is one quarter note as a pickup, there will be two quarter notes in the last measure.

**Clap and Count Out Loud**

Book 2
Track 26

Count: (1  2  3)  4    1  2  3  4    1  2  3  4    1  2  3  4    1  2  3  (4)

# A-Tisket, A-Tasket

Book 2
Track 27
Vocals & Chords

Book 2
Track 28
Chords Only

95

# ACTIVITY: Pickup Measures

## Counting Time

For each example, write the counts for the pickup measure and the final measure under the staff. Put parentheses around the counts that aren't played.

(1) (2) (3) 4          1  2  3  (4)

___  ___  ___          ___  ___  ___

___  ___  ___  ___          ___  ___  ___

___  ___  ___          ___  ___  ___

___  ___  ___  ___          ___  ___  ___

# Tom Dooley

Book 2
Track 29
Vocals & Chords

Book 2
Track 30
Chords Only

**Moderately slow**

Hang down your head, Tom Doo - ley. _____

Hang down your head and cry. _____

Hang down your head, Tom Doo - ley. _____

Poor boy, you're bound to die. _____

# Eighth Notes

*Eighth notes* are black notes with a flag added to the stem: ♪ or ♩ .

Two or more eighth notes are written with beams: ♫ or ♫ , ♬ or ♬ .

Each eighth note receives one half beat.

| WHOLE NOTE | 2 HALF NOTES | 4 QUARTER NOTES | 8 EIGHTH NOTES |

Use alternating downstrokes ⊓ and upstrokes ∨ on eighth notes.

Book 2
Track 31

COUNT:  1  &  2  &  3  &  4  &     1  &  2  &  3  &  4  &

# Jammin' with Eighth Notes

Book 2
Track 32
Melody & Chords

Book 2
Track 33
Chords Only

*Allegro moderato means moderately fast.

# ACTIVITY: The Eighth Note

An *eighth note* has a black notehead, a stem, and a flag. Each eighth note equals half a beat.

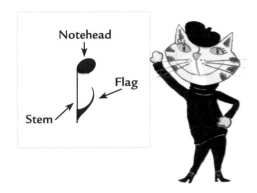

## How to Draw the Eighth Note

**Step 1:** Draw a quarter note.

**Step 2:** Draw the flag up from the bottom of the stem that look like the leaf of a flower.

Now, draw six eighth notes on the third space of the staff.

Now, draw six eighth notes in the second space with the stem going up from the right of the notehead, and the flag going down instead of up.

## Beaming Eighth Notes

Draw eight eighth notes in each measure and beam the notes in groups of four ( ♫♫ ). In the first measure, draw eighth notes having stems down, and in the second measure, draw eighth notes having stems up. Then, write the counts below the staff.

99

# Go Tell Aunt Rhody

Book 2
Track 34
Vocals & Chords

Book 2
Track 35
Chords Only

**Moderato**

Go tell Aunt Rho - dy, go tell Aunt Rho - dy,

go tell Aunt Rho - dy that the old gray goose is dead. The

one we've been sav - ing, the one we've been sav - ing, the

one we've been sav - ing to make a feath - er bed.

100

# Love Somebody (Extended Version)

Book 2

Track 36
Vocals & Chords

Book 2

Track 37
Chords Only

**Moderately**

Love some-bod-y, yes, I do; Love some-bod-y, yes, I do;

Love some-bod-y, yes, I do; Love some-bod-y, but I won't tell who.

Love some-bod-y, yes, I do; Love some-bod-y, yes, I do;

Love some-bod-y, yes, I do; And I hope some-bod-y loves me too.

# Clementine

Book 2

 Track 38
Vocals & Chords

Book 2

Track 39
Chords Only

**Moderately fast**

In a cav - ern, in a can - yon, ex - ca - vat - ing for a

mine, lived a min - er, for - ty - nin - er, and his

daugh - ter, Clem - en - tine. Oh my dar - lin', oh my

dar - lin', oh my dar - lin', Clem - en - tine, you are

lost and gone for - ev - er; Dread-ful sor - ry, Clem-en - tine.

## Additional Verses

*Verse 2*
Light she was and like a fairy,
And her shoes were number nine,
Herring boxes, without topses,
Sandals were for Clementine.

*Chorus*
Oh my darlin', oh my darlin',
Oh my darlin' Clementine!
You art lost and gone forever
Dreadful sorry, Clementine.

*Verse 3*
Drove she ducklings to the water
Every morning just at nine,
Hit her foot against a splinter,
Fell into the foaming brine.

*Chorus*
Oh my darlin', oh my darlin',
Oh my darlin' Clementine!
You art lost and gone forever
Dreadful sorry, Clementine.

*Verse 4*
Ruby lips above the water,
Blowing bubbles soft and fine,
But, alas, I was no swimmer,
So I lost my Clementine.

*Chorus*
Oh my darlin', oh my darlin',
Oh my darlin' Clementine!
You art lost and gone forever
Dreadful sorry, Clementine.

# Dotted Quarter Notes

**A DOT INCREASES THE LENGTH OF A NOTE BY ONE HALF**

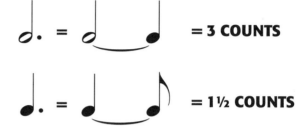

## Counting Dotted Quarter Notes

The only difference in the following two measures and those directly above them is the way they are written. They should sound the same.

## Cockles and Mussels

Book 2  Track 40 Vocals & Chords

Book 2  Track 41 Chords Only

In Dub - lin's fair cit - y, where girls are so pret-ty, I

first set my eyes on sweet Mol - ly Ma - lone, As she

wheeled her    wheel- bar-row    through   streets broad    and    nar-row,      cry - ing

Cock - les     and    Mus-sels!    A - live,     a - live,    oh!

A - live,     a - live,    oh! __    A - live,    al - live,    oh! __    Cry-ing

Cock - les     and    Mus-sels!    A - live,     a - live,    oh!

# ACTIVITY:
# The Dotted Quarter Note

The *dotted quarter note* lasts 1½ beats.

## How to Draw the Dotted Quarter Note

**Step 1:** Draw a quarter note.

**Step 2:** Add a dot to the right of the notehead.

Now, draw three dotted quarter notes with stems going up and three dotted quarter notes with stems going down.

## Write the Number of Beats

Here are all the types of notes, slashes, and rests you know so far. Write the number of beats each symbol receives (1, 2, 3, 4, one half, or 1 ½) on the line below the staff.

106

# Dynamics

Symbols that show how loud or soft to play are called *dynamics*. These symbols come from Italian words. Four of the most common dynamics are shown here.

| **_p_** | **_mf_** | **_f_** | **_ff_** |
|---|---|---|---|
| *piano* | *mezzo-forte* | *forte* | *fortissimo* |
| ("PYAH-noh") | ("MED-zoh FOHR-teh") | ("FOHR-teh") | ("fohr-TEE-see-moh") |
| **soft** | **moderately loud** | **loud** | **very loud** |

## Echo Rock

Book 2 — Track 42 — Melody & Chords

Book 2 — Track 43 — Chords Only

# The Streets of Laredo

Book 2

 Track 44
Vocals & Chords

Book 2

 Track 45
Chords Only

**Moderately**

PLAY:

As I_____ walked out in the streets of La - re - do, as

I walked out in La - re - do one day, I

spied a young cow - boy all dressed in white lin - en, all

dressed in white lin - en as cold as the clay.

Book 2
Track 46

# The Down-and-Up Stroke

You can make your accompaniment of waltz songs in $\frac{3}{4}$ like "The Streets of Laredo" more interesting by replacing the second beat of the measure with a downstroke followed by an upstroke. The symbol for downstroke is ⊓; an upstroke uses the symbol V. Together, the down-and-up strokes are two eighth notes that are played in the same time as single quarter note.

Try the following exercise to first just work on the new rhythm.

Now practice changing from C to G7.

Now practice changing back and forth from C to G7 and back. When you can do it smoothly, go back to page 31 and use it to accompany "The Streets of Laredo."

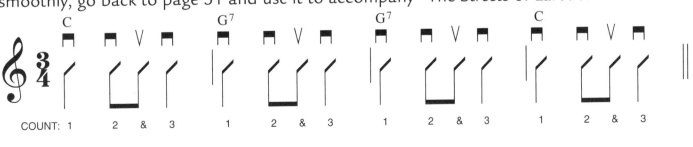

In $\frac{4}{4}$ time, use the pattern ⊓ ⊓ V ⊓ ⊓ V .

# ACTIVITY: Dynamics

*Dynamics* are symbols that tell you how loud or soft to play. Below are the four most common dynamics.

**p** stands for *piano*, which means **soft**.

**mf** stands for *mezzo-forte*, which means **moderately loud**.

**f** stands for *forte*, which means **loud**.

**ff** stands for *fortissimo*, which means **very loud**.

## Writing Dynamics

Write the correct dynamic sign next to its definition.

loud _____

soft _____

very loud _____

moderately loud _____

# ACTIVITY: The Downstroke and Upstroke

Draw the symbol for the downstroke ⊓ six times above these notes.

Draw the symbol for the upstroke V six times above these notes.

## The Fermata

This sign is called a *fermata*. It means to hold the note it is over a little longer.

Book 2

Track 47
Vocals & Chords

Book 2

Track 48
Chords Only

# Michael, Row the Boat Ashore

**Moderately slow and steady**

Mi - chael, row the boat a - shore, hal - le -

lu - jah! Mi - chael, row the boat a -

shore, hal - le - lu - jah!

# ACTIVITY: The Fermata

A *fermata* means to play the note a little longer than normal (usually about twice the normal length). The fermata is sometimes called a "bird's eye."

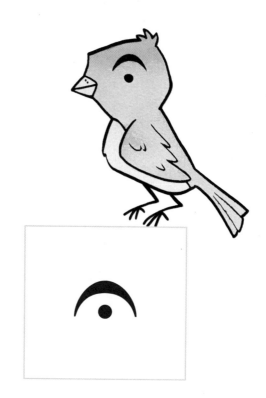

## Drawing the Fermata

**Step 1:** Draw the top half of a circle above the note.

**Step 2:** Place a dot inside the half circle.

Now, draw a fermata over each of the notes below.

# Introducing F-sharp

A *sharp* ♯ raises a note a half step. F♯ is played one fret higher than the note F. When a sharp note appears in a measure, it is still sharp until the end of that measure.

**Hear this note!**
Book 2

Track 49

## Little Brown Jug

Book 2
Track 50
Vocals & Chords

Book 2
Track 51
Chords Only

# ACTIVITY: The Note F-sharp

The note with a sharp sign on the bottom space of the staff is called F♯.

## Drawing the Note F-sharp

To draw the note F♯ on the staff, place the notehead in the bottom space, and draw the stem up to the top line. Then draw a sharp sign ♯ to the left of the notehead. A sharp sign is like a small tic-tac-toe symbol. On the staff below, draw the note F♯ six times.

## Playing the Note F♯

To play the note F♯, press the 2nd string at the 2nd fret.

On the diagram to the right, indicate the fingering for the note F♯ by placing the number "2" in a circle on the 2nd fret of the 2nd string.

## Write Your Own Melody with the Notes C, D, E, F-sharp, G, A, B, and C

Compose a short melody with the notes C, D, E, F-sharp, G, A, B, and C. Use eighth notes, quarter notes, dotted quarter notes, half notes, dotted half notes, and whole notes. Also included dynamics and a tempo sign. Remember that in $\frac{4}{4}$ time, only four beats fit in each measure.

# The G Chord

  Track 52

**G**

Place your 1st, 2nd, and 3rd fingers in position, then play one string at a time.

Play all four strings together:

 +  +  +  =

**G Chord**

# The D7 Chord

 Track 53

**D7**

Place your 1st and 2nd fingers in position, then play one string at a time.

Play all four strings together:

 +  +  +  =

115

# Over the Rainbow (Extended Version)

The greatest ukulele version of this song was recorded in
1993 by legendary Hawaiian uke player and singer Iz.

**Words by E. Y. Harburg**
**Music by Harold Arlen**

day I'll wish up-on a star and wake up where the clouds are far be-hind me._____ Where

trou-bles melt like lem-on drops, a - way a-bove the chim-ney tops that's where you'll find me.

Some - where    o - ver the rain-bow    blue - birds    fly,

birds    fly    o - ver the rain-bow    why then,oh why can't    I?

# ACTIVITY:
## The G and D7 Chords

**The G Chord**

G

Write the chord symbol
"G" three times.

_____

_____

_____

**The D7 Chord**

D7

Write the chord symbol
"D7" three times.

D⁷

_____

_____

_____

Finish drawing the **o**'s and fingering for the chords below.

G

D⁷

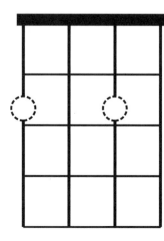

# ACTIVITY:
## Review: All the Notes and Chords You Learned in Books 1 & 2

Write the letter name of each note in the box below the staff.

Write the name of each chord in the box above the chord diagram.

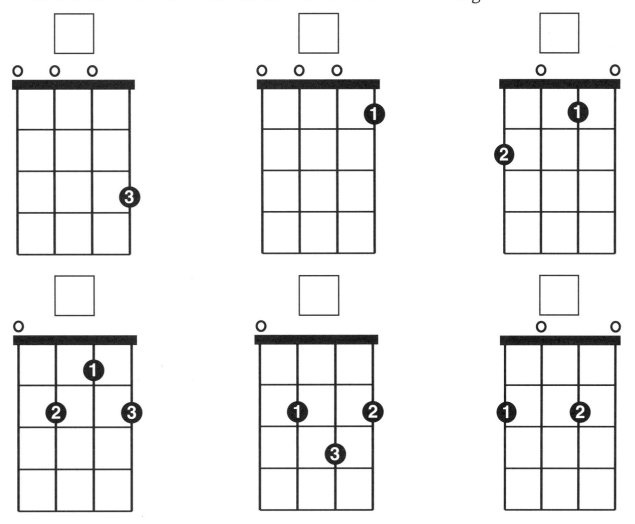

# Review: Music Matching Games

## Chords

Draw a line to match each chord frame on the left to the correct photo on the right.

1.  F    

2.  C⁷    

3.  C

4.  G⁷    

5.  G    

6. D⁷

## Symbols

Draw a line to match each symbol on the left to its name on the right.

1.      Dotted half note

2. $\frac{3}{4}$     Whole rest

3. 𝅘𝅥     Tie

4. *ff*     Three beats in a measure

    𝅗𝅥.     Fermata

5. ▬     

6. *Moderato*     Common time

7. *mf*     Loud

8. **C**     Moderately loud

9. *Allegro*     Soft

10. *p*     Very loud

11. *Andante*     Slow

12. ⌢     Moderately

13. *f*     Fast

## Notes

Draw a line to match each note on the left to its correct music notation on the right.

1.     

2.     

3.     

4.     

5.     

6.     

7.     

8.     

9.     

10.     

## Answer Key

**Chords**
1: page 23; 2: page 20; 3: page 16; 4: page 31, 5: page 115; 6: page 115

**Symbols**
1: page 90; 2: page 77; 3: page 77; 4: page 107; 5: page 57; 6: page 86; 7: page 107; 8: page 81; 9: page 86; 10: page 107; 11: page 86; 12: page 111; 13: page 107

**Notes**
1: page 49; 2: page 52; 3: page 43; 4: page 68; 5: page 55; 6: page 59; 7: page 46; 8: page 64; 9: page 83; 10: page 113;